Explode The Code

Essential lessons for phonics mastery

2nd Edition

1

Nancy Hall • Rena Price

EDUCATORS PUBLISHING SERVICE
Cambridge and Toronto

Cover art: Hugh Price
Text illustrations: Laura Price, Alan Price, Kelly Kennedy

Printed in Mayfield, PA, in July 2020
ISBN 978-0-8388-7801-9

7 8 9 10 PAH 23 22 21 20

Consonant Pretest

(See Teacher's Key for Books 1 to 5.)

◯ it.

f			
k			
r			
t			
l			
g			

i

Consonant Pretest

( ) it.

v			
h			
s			
d			
j			
z			
c			

Consonant Pretest

b			
w			
m			
y			
p			
qu			
n			

*For further practice with consonants, see Primers for the Explode The Code series.

Lesson 1

a says /ă/ as in

Find the picture that begins with the sound of the letter below.

( ) it.

ă			
ă	$+ \dfrac{2}{\ \ 2\ \ }{4}$		
ă			
ă			
ă			
ă			

1

bat	hat	(bat)
fat	hat	fat
mat	mat	nat
pat	bat	pat
rat	rap	rat
cat	cot	cat
sat	sat	sap

2

Follow the arrows to write the letter **a,** which says /ă/ as in 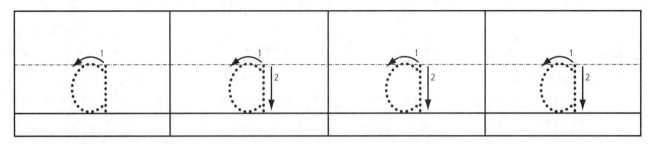.
Say the sound aloud. Notice that **a** begins like the letter **c.**

Notice that **a** is only one space tall. Trace the letters.

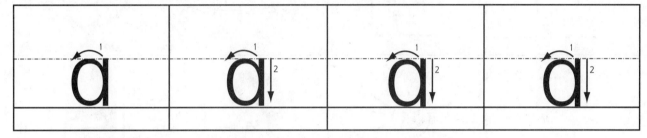

Trace and copy the letter that begins the pictured word.

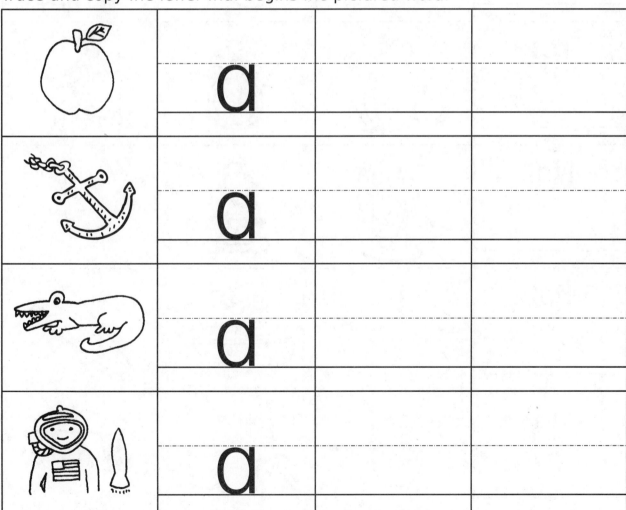

Read, copy, and ⬭ it.

bat **b a t**			
hat — — —			
sat — — —			
rat — — —			
Nat — — —			
bat — — —			
mat — — —			

Spell.   Write.

	(b) g	(a) n	f (t)	**bat**
	s r	n a	t m	
	h b	o a	t p	
	g p	a x	t d	
	w m	i a	k t	
	c d	m a	t h	
	p b	a r	t d	

5

Match and write it.

| hat | b̶a̶t̶ | mat | bat |
| pat | rat | sat | cat |

bat	

6

◯ it.

bad

fat

(bat)

rat
ran
tar

can
cat
cab

nap
tan
Nat

man
tam
mat

pat
bat
pad

cat
sad
sat

7

X it.

The hat is fat.	☐	
The bat is fat.	☒	
Pat sat on a cat.	☐	
Pat sat on a mat.	☐	
A cat is at bat.	☐	
A rat is at bat.	☐	
The cat is on a mat.	☐	
The rat is on a cat.	☐	
Nat sat at bat.	☐	
Nat sat on a rat.	☐	
A fat bat is on a cat.	☐	
A fat cat is on a hat.	☐	
The rat sat.	☐	
The bat sat.	☐	

Write it.

bat

Lesson 2

a says /ă/ as in

Find the picture that begins with
the sound of the letter below.

⬭ it.

ă			
ă			
ă			
ă			
ă			
ă			

10

◯ the same word.

fan	ban	(fan)
can	con	can
had	lad	had
ran	ram	ran
tan	nat	tan
bad	dad	bad
pan	pan	ban

Read, copy, and ◯ it.

fan **f a n**			
can ___ ___ ___			
dad ___ ___ ___			
Pam ___ ___ ___			
mad ___ ___ ___			
cat ___ ___ ___			
ran ___ ___ ___			

	(f) l (a) c i (n)	**fan**
	m n a d m n	
	k s c a d g	
	r w a k n t	
	p v g a d n	
	r j c a t n	
	t h a c t m	

13

it.

 fat （fan） man	

dad had bat		jam Jan tap	
can cat car		dad bat tab	
fad sat sad		fan rat ran	

Match and write it.

| fan | hat | bat | can |
| pan | man | mad | sad |

fan

X it.

The cat is fat.	☒	
A rat is sad.	☐	
The cat is mad.	☐	
The hat is mad.	☐	
The fan ran.	☐	
The man ran.	☐	
The mat is sad.	☐	
The rat is sad.	☐	
Sam has a can.	☐	
Sam has a cat.	☐	
The fat rat bats.	☐	
Pat is at bat.	☐	
The can sat in the pan.	☐	
The man had a fan.	☐	

Write it.

fan

Lesson 3

a says /ă/ as in

Find the picture that begins with
the sound of the letter below.

◯ it.

ă			
ă			$\begin{array}{r} 2 \\ +\ 2 \\ \hline 4 \end{array}$
ă			
ă			
ă			
ă			

⬭ the same word.

bag	gab	(bag)
gas	gab	gas
ban	dan	ban
had	had	hag
fad	lad	fad
map	nap	map
jam	jan	jam

Read, copy, and ⬭ it.

bag **b a g**			
pal ___ ___ ___			
cap ___ ___ ___			
tag ___ ___ ___			
fan ___ ___ ___			
rat ___ ___ ___			
wag ___ ___ ___			

	Spell.			Write.
	(b) g	c (a)	(g) j	**bag**
	r n	a o	p t	
	m w	a c	p t	
	g d	b a	n s	
	f t	d a	n m	
	r n	c a	b t	
	g c	a o	m p	

21

it.

bad

(bag)

gab

sap
pass
pan

Al
at
am

sag
sap
nap

tap
tag
hag

pad
pan
pal

mitt
mat
sat

Match and write it.

sat   nap   wag   b~~a~~g

mat   Pam   gas   tag

bag

X it.

A rat naps in a cap. The man pats a cat.	☒ ☐	
Sam has a bag. The rat is in the van.	☐ ☐	
A bass is at bat. A cat is at bat.	☐ ☐	
Pat has a nap. Pat has a fan.	☐ ☐	
A rat sat on Pam. A cat sat in a bag.	☐ ☐	
Al has a cap. Al has a pal.	☐ ☐	
The bat can wag. The hat has a tag.	☐ ☐	

24

Write it.

bag

Lesson 4

i says /ĭ/ as in

Find the picture that begins with
the sound of the letter below.

 it.

ĭ			
ĭ			
ĭ			
ĭ			
ĭ			
ĭ			

26

Follow the arrows to write the letter **i,** which says /ĭ/ as in 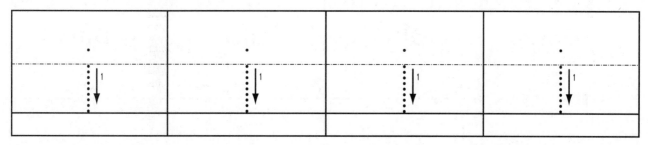.
Say the sound aloud.

Notice that **i** is only one space tall. Trace the letters.

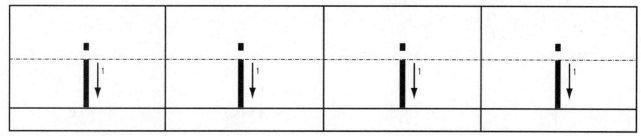

Trace and copy the letter that begins the pictured word.

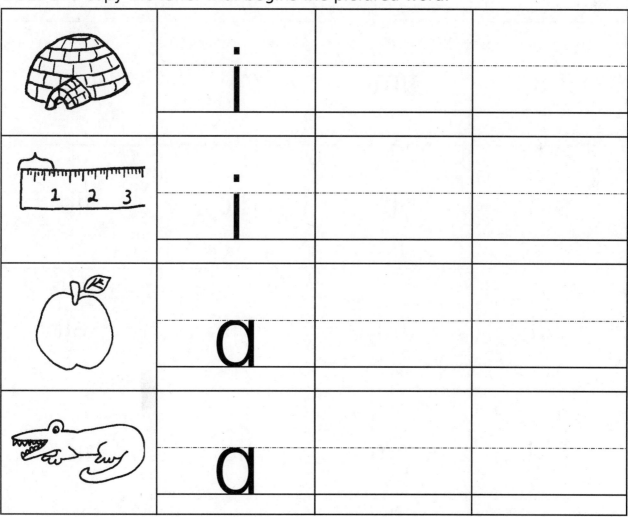

27

$\bigcirc$ the same word.

bill	pin	din	$\widehat{bill}$
fit	lit	fit	fill
his	sit	his	has
tin	tim	nit	tin
did	bid	did	bib
Jill	Jill	Till	Jell
hid	mid	lid	hid

Read, copy, and ◯ it.

pig **pig**			
hill — — — —			
wig — — — —	$+\dfrac{\begin{array}{r}2\\2\end{array}}{4}$		
Jim — — — —			
bit — — — —			
win — — — —			
dig — — — —			

29

Match and write it.

pig	win	wig	~~lip~~
mitt	fin	sit	pin

lip

_____

_____

_____

_____

_____

Spell.   Write.

	(h) b	a (i) m	(ll)	**hill**
	b p	i j	g p	
	m n	i a	tt l	
	d b	n i	p g	
	b d	i j	t k	
	w m	i t	g p	
	n p	i a	n m	

◯ it.

sad

sit

(sip)

hit
hat
hill

dig
bib
big

hat
fill
fin

wit
sit
sill

mat
mitt
mill

fill
hit
hill

32

X it.

A pig is big. A pin is big.	☐ ☒	
Lin bit the can. Lin hit the can.	☐ ☐	
The man can dig. The man can sit.	☐ ☐	
The fin is big. The pin is big.	☐ ☐	
Pam has a big pig. Pam has a bad wig.	☐ ☐	
Jim sits on a pin. Jim sat on a van.	☐ ☐	
Pat has big hats. Pat has a big mitt.	☐ ☐	

Write it.

hill

*For further practice on short *i*, see Book 1½, pp. 9–16.

Lesson 5 • Review Lesson

Find the picture that begins with the sound of each letter below. ⬭ it.

ă = (apple)   ĭ = (igloo)

ă			
ĭ			
ă			
ĭ			
ă			
ĭ			

35

◯ the same word.

pan	pin	(pan)	din
wig	wig	wag	wit
lid	lad	lid	lib
dad	dad	dab	bad
sat	sit	sat	sad
tin	tan	tin	nit
has	his	has	hag

36

Read, copy, and ⬭ it.

pan			
p a n			
bag			
_ _ _			
win			
_ _ _			
wig			
_ _ _			
mad			
_ _ _			
sip			
_ _ _			
lip			
_ _ _			

37

Spell.   Write.

	b (p) (a) i m (n)			**pan**
	l f i a n m			
	b d i a p g			
	w m a i q g			
	l t i a t p			
	p w a i t n			
	l s a i p d			

it.

pin

fan

(pan)

bat
tab
bit

hill
Jill
jam

odd
add
ill

$2 + 2 = 4$

wig
wag
bag

ball
bit
Bill

bib
lap
big

39

X it.

The mat is big. The wig is big.	☐ ☒	
Bill can add. His hat is a lid.	☐ ☐	
Dad has a big pin. Dad has big lips.	☐ ☐	
The cat has a fan. The cap has a fin.	☐ ☐	
Jill has a big mitt. Jill sits on a mat.	☐ ☐	
The big rat wins. The rat sips jam.	☐ ☐	
Pat has a big pig. A tin pig bit Pat.	☐ ☐	

40

Write it.

pan

*For further practice on short *a* in combination, see Book 1½, pp. 17–24.

41

u says /ŭ/ as in

Find the picture that begins with
the sound of the letter below.

◯ it.

ŭ			
ŭ			
ŭ			
ŭ			
ŭ			
ŭ			

⬭ the same word.

hug	dug	(hug)	bug
rub	rib	rut	rub
hum	hum	ham	mum
fun	fan	hum	fun
tug	lug	tug	tag
gum	mug	bug	gum
but	but	tub	bat

Read, copy, and ⬭ it.

hug **h u g**			
bug ___ ___ ___			
sub ___ ___ ___			
run ___ ___ ___			
rug ___ ___ ___			
pup ___ ___ ___			
bus ___ ___ ___			

Follow the arrows to write the letter **u,** which says /ŭ/ as in .
Say the sound aloud.

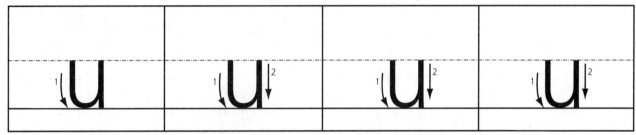

Notice that **u** is only one space tall. Trace the letters.

Trace and copy the letter that begins the pictured word.

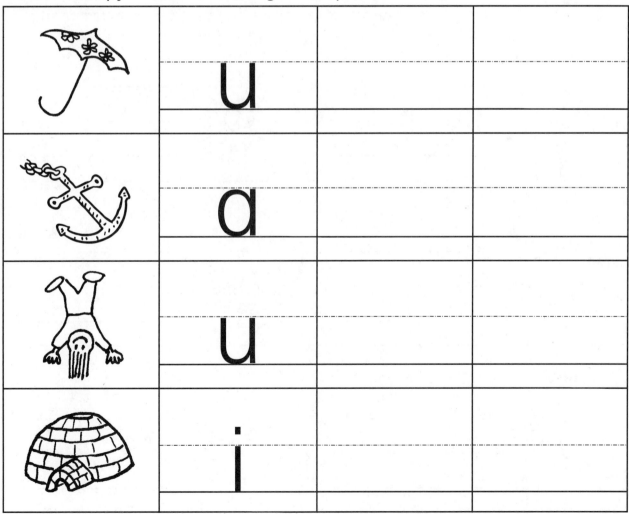

Match and write it.

rug   ~~hug~~   sun   gum

bus   bug   run   cup

hug

_____

_____

_____

_____

_____

_____

Spell. Write.

b (h) (u) a p (g)				**hug**
p g u n b p				_ _ _ _ _
a s u a m n				_ _ _ _ _
p b n u c s				_ _ _ _ _
g p a u n m				_ _ _ _ _
o c n u b p				_ _ _ _ _
b d u a p g				_ _ _ _ _

47

it.

hum

hug

dug

mug
pan
gum

pub
pup
bug

rug
rag
mug

hut
hat
nut

sup
sip
sub

tub
tug
lug

X it.

The pup dug in the sun. The cat sat in the sun.	☒ ☐	
A bug is in the mud. A bug is on Jim.	☐ ☐	
The pup hid in the hut. The bus hid in the hut.	☐ ☐	
A tug is on the rug. Tim can tug and tug.	☐ ☐	
The sun is on the rug. The bug is in the sun.	☐ ☐	
The sub is in the mud. The tub is in the sun.	☐ ☐	
The pup sits on the cup. A cup is on the hut.	☐ ☐	

Write it.

hug

*For further practice on short *u*, see Book 1½, pp. 25–32.

Find the picture that begins with
the sound of each letter below.
⬭ it.

ă			
ĭ			
ŭ			
ĭ			
ŭ			
ă			

Read, copy, and ◯ it.

nut **n u t**			
fill ___ ___ ___ ___			
Ann ___ ___ ___			
bun ___ ___ ___			
mug ___ ___ ___			
cap ___ ___ ___			
tub ___ ___ ___			

52

Spell.   Write.

	(n) s	(u) n	(t) l	nut
	m n	i e	t x	
	t f	u a	d b	
	r c	u a	g p	
	u m	i u	g b	
	b d	u a	n u	
	f t	i e	ll tt	

53

Match and write it.

six	fill	cut	Dan
mix	duck	~~nut~~	fix

nut

Yes or no?

	Yes	No
Can I fill a cup up?	☐	☒
Will a duck pass a bus?	☐	☐
Will a sick cat nap a bit?	☐	☐
Can a pig add six and six?	☐	☐
Is it fun to pick nuts?	☐	☐
Can a bag rip?	☐	☐
Can a bug hug a rat?	☐	☐

nat

mutt

(nut)

cat
cut
cup

nix
max
mix

mitt
nut
mutt

bed
bud
bad

fix
tax
fin

duck
luck
back

X it.

A big mutt naps. It is a big mug.	☐ ☒	
The bug is on a hill. The sub is on a hill.	☐ ☐	
Bill sat on a mutt. Bill sat in the bus.	☐ ☐	
A cat hid the nut. A rat wins a cup.	☐ ☐	
Ann has a mitt. Sam will mix the nuts.	☐ ☐	
Jill naps in the bus. Jill hid in the tub.	☐ ☐	
Jan can fix the bus. Jan can fit a bun in the bag.	☐ ☐	

Write it.

nut

*For further practice on short *a, i,* and *u,* see Book 1½, pp. 33–48.

Lesson 8

e says /ĕ/ as in

Find the picture that begins with
the sound of the letter below.
◯ it.

ĕ			
ĕ			
ĕ			
ĕ			
ĕ			
ĕ			

59

◯ the same word.

pen	pan	(pen)	hen
let	led	lit	let
well	well	will	mill
red	reb	ned	red
beg	bag	beg	bug
led	leg	lid	led
pep	peg	pep	pip

60

Follow the arrows to write the letter **e,** which says /ĕ/ as in .
Say the sound aloud.

e	e	e	e

Notice that **e** is only one space tall. Trace the letters.

e	e	e	e

Trace and copy the letter that begins the pictured word.

	e		
	e		
	u		
	e		

Read, copy, and ⬭ it.

pen p e n			
net _ _ _ _			
ten _ _ _ _			
fell _ _ _ _			
hen _ _ _ _			
Peg _ _ _ _			
bell _ _ _ _			

Spell.   Write.

	(p) b	a (e)	(n) m	**pen**
10	i t	a e	m n	
	d b	e n	p d	
	l h	a e	g p	
	n m	e a	t l	
	h t	e i	m n	
	b d	e i	ll tt	

63

Match and write it.

bed   Ted   leg   bell

fed   ~~pen~~   met   net

pen

◯ it.

hen

(pen)

pan

led
fed
leg

mitt
miss
mess

kit
bet
pet

sip
sell
fell

Nan
men
mum

met
mat
net

X it.

A wet hen sits. The pen is wet.	☐ ☒	
Nan fell in the pen. Nan fed the pet.	☐ ☐	
The pet has a fin. The net has a rip.	☐ ☐	
Ten men fed the hen. Al met a fat hen.	☐ ☐	
Peg fell in the tub. Peg will tug the bell.	☐ ☐	
His bed is a mess. Six men sit on a bus.	☐ ☐	
The bugs fed the duck. Pam digs and digs.	☐ ☐	

Write it.

pen

Lesson 9 • Review Lesson

Find the picture that begins with
the sound of each letter below.
⬭ it.

68

◯ the same word.

tip	lip	(tip)	tap
hum	ham	hug	hum
jug	jag	jug	jab
kid	hip	hid	kid
Sal	Sat	Sell	Sal
get	get	gut	gal
sis	sip	sis	sit

Read, copy, and ◯ it.

tip t i p			
six ___ ___ ___		**6**	
fun ___ ___ ___			
beg ___ ___ ___			
Kim ___ ___ ___			
web ___ ___ ___			
Jeff ___ ___ ___			JAM

70

	k	(t) a	(i) b	(p)	**tip**
	w	p e	u g	b	
	d	l e	a g	p	
	m	n i	u t	l	
	m	b a	e t	g	
	h	s i	u d	p	
	m	z i	e p	n	

Match and write it.

Kim	beg	wet	nut
~~tip~~	fell	hid	zip

tip

_____

_____

_____

_____

_____

_____

( ) it.

tim

(tip)

top

	wed		hip
	web		nap
	wet		net

	met		Deb
	wet		fed
	wit		bed

	six		bed
	zip		bid
	set		bud

73

Peg is ten. The can is tin.	☒ ☐	
Jen will tip the big can. Jen will pass the nuts.	☐ ☐	
Ted tips the cup. Ted met his pal.	☐ ☐	
Kim hid in a jug. Kim hugs the pet.	☐ ☐	
A big, wet bag fell. A bug sat in the web.	☐ ☐	
Deb has ten legs. Deb has fun.	☐ ☐	
The big pup begs us. The pup tips its hat.	☐ ☐	

Write it.

tip

*For further practice on short *a*, *i*, *u*, and *e* combined, see Book 1½, pp. 57–64.

75

Lesson 10

o says /ŏ/ as in

Find the picture that begins with
the sound of each letter below.

⬭ it.

ŏ			
ă			
ŏ			
ĭ			
ŏ			
ĕ			

76

Follow the arrows to write the letter **o,** which says /ŏ/ as in .
Say the sound aloud.

Notice that **o** is only one space tall. Trace the letters.

Trace and copy the letter that begins the pictured word.

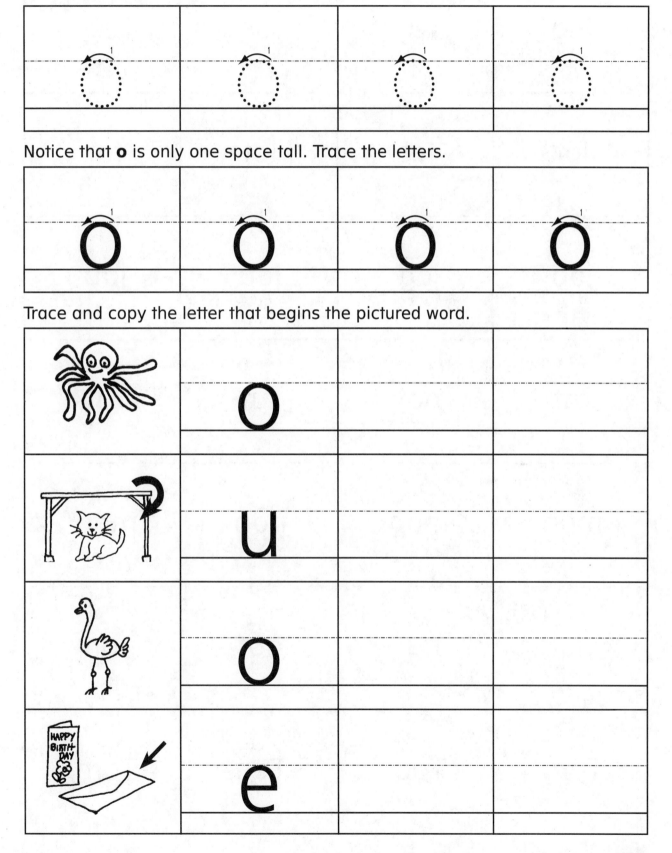

the same word.

log	leg	fog	(log)
lot	let	lot	tot
job	jog	job	jab
rot	not	rut	rot
mob	mob	nob	mad
not	nut	not	ton
Tom	Tod	Ton	Tom

Read, copy, and ⬭ it.

log **l o g**			
fox ___ ___ ___			
cop ___ ___ ___			
Rob ___ ___ ___			
top ___ ___ ___			
mom ___ ___ ___			
pot ___ ___ ___			

Match and write it.

rip   pot   mom   ~~log~~

rod   mop   hop   box

log

Spell.   Write.

	l t a o p g			**log**
	b d o a n x			
	m n o a n m			
	p d o a t l			
	f t o u x n			
	r n a o b d			
	c t o u p b			

81

it.

lug
(log)
leg

hop
tot
hot

mop
map
nap

rib
rub
Rob

hog
nap
hop

Bob
bib
bed

dug
dog
fog

X it.

A cat is in a hot tub.	☒	
A log is in a pot.	☐	
Jill pats the wet dog.	☐	
Jill has a hot dog.	☐	
The cop sits on a box.	☐	
The cop sits on a fox.	☐	
Pam fills the pot.	☐	
Pam can sit on the log.	☐	
The dog is on the box.	☐	
The box is on the dog.	☐	
The mop will fix the mess.	☐	
The pig sits in the mess.	☐	
The pup sits on the hog.	☐	
The fox hops on the log.	☐	

Write it.

log

*For further practice on short *o*, see Book 1½, pp. 65–72.

Find the picture that begins with
the sound of each letter below.

it.

ĕ	$+\dfrac{\begin{array}{r}2\\2\end{array}}{4}$		
ŏ			
ă			
ĭ			
ŭ			
ĕ			

⬭ the same word.

rat	cat	(rat)	rag
pop	pep	pop	pup
pack	pick	pack	peck
led	lid	led	lad
sick	sack	sick	sock
rock	rock	rack	mock
luck	lock	tuck	luck

86

Match and write it.

bib   ~~rat~~   duck   kick

well   lock   neck   doll

rat

Spell.   Write.

	c (r) (a) o f (t)			**rat**
	n m e	i b ck		_____
	m w e	i ck ll		_____
	t k i	e ck ss		_____
	l t a	o z ck		_____
	b d o	u ck g		_____
	d b e	o ll ck		_____

Yes or no?

	Yes	No
Can Jim sip pop?	☐	☒
Can a doll run?	☐	☐
Will Jill sit on a rat?	☐	☐
Can a duck get a wig?	☐	☐
Can a well kick?	☐	☐
Will a hat fit Jeff?	☐	☐
Will a big tub hop?	☐	☐

X it.

It is a big lock. Dot has a red sock.	☒ ☐	
The pig led Jim to the box. The pig locks Jim in the bus.	☐ ☐	
The men sell a hen in a pen. The duck met a cat at the well.	☐ ☐	
Pat fell and hit his leg. Pam kicks a can on the hill.	☐ ☐	
Jill sits on a wet duck. Jeff has a wet bug on his back.	☐ ☐	
The mutt has a bell on its neck. The mutt met a duck on a log.	☐ ☐	
Bill will lock the dog pen. Bill kicks the bag of rags.	☐ ☐	

Write it.

rat

Write it.

*For further practice, see Book 1½, pp. 73–88.

1.	hop hip hog	2.	wed web wet
3.	sill fill hill	4.	cup cap cop
5.	dad bad dab	6.	bug big beg
7.	his him hum	8.	mat men met

1.

2.

3.

4.

5.

Read and ⬭ it.

1. A hen can	red. run. rut.
2. I can sip from a	cub. cud. cup.
3. The sun is big and	hit. hat. hot.
4. The rug has a	rap. rip. rod.
5. An ax can cut a	log. lag. lug.
6. I will nap on a	bud. bed. bid.

Read and ⬭ it.

1. I can sit and run and beg. I can
    dig up a rib and tug on a mat.
    I am a pal and a pet. I am a

    pop.

    pup.

    pep.

2. Tom will fill it and mix in it. Tom
    has ham in it and a lid on top. If it
    tips, it is a mess! It is a

    pet.

    pit.

    pot.